1,000 REASONS YOU'RE MY FRIEND

1,000 REASONS YOU'RE MY FRIEND

Michael Powell

Andrews McMeel
Publishing

Kansas City

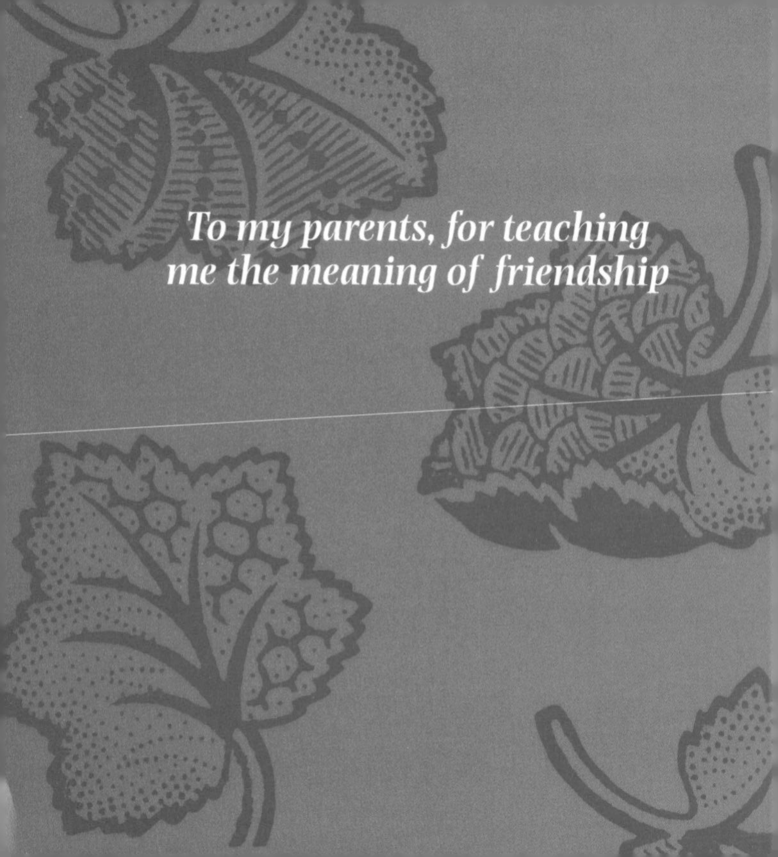

To my parents, for teaching me the meaning of friendship

Contents

Introduction

What is friendship? What is the nature of this special bond that defines our identities, shapes our experiences, and grows stronger with every minute that passes?

Sometimes friendship can seem fraught with contradictions: It is constant and changeable, inviting both curiosity and familiarity; it is challenging and relaxing. It demands honesty, trust, and commitment while offering guidance, inspiration, and delight. It always sustains us through hard times and nourishes us in times of plenty, and it can open a heart faster than a key can open a door.

But what does true friendship really mean? How does it develop and how does it change? How do our friends behave and what do they make us feel?

Within these pages we shall explore all the gifts that friendship brings and reveal how friends enrich our lives—helping us to interpret our past, shape our future, and enjoy living in the moment.

1

What Is Friendship?

Friendship is two snowflakes melting side by side.

Friendship is the sunbeam that pierces the forest canopy to warm the earth.

Friendship is a mystic dance in which we must supply the music.

"It's **not** something you learn in school. But if you **haven't** learned the meaning of friendship, you **really haven't** learned anything."

Muhammad Ali

A friend is someone who gives you the total freedom to reinvent yourself.

Friends never say "You wouldn't understand."

Friendships are sewn one stitch at a time.

Long **before** we are even **ready** or **aware** of it, friendship can **transform** us.

Being someone's friend is a voyage you map out as you go along.

Friendship is God's **special** way of **loving** us through **someone else**.

"Best friend, my well-spring in the wilderness!"

George Eliot

Friendship is like a home—it doesn't just happen; it is built and furnished.

You **cannot** collect **all** the beautiful shells on the beach; pick **one** or **two** of the **best** and take them home.

Friendship is the light under heaven's door.

Friendship is a sidewalk in the middle of the fast lane.

The gift that never stops giving—friendship.

Friendship is a ticker-tape parade for two.

Friendship gives a tiny clue to what the whole world could do.

True friendship is never broken, weakened, or strained; it's simply tested.

Friendship should be the inspiration for all acts of creation.

We get the friends that we deserve, and, if we are lucky, a few that we don't.

Friendship can develop in foxholes or in chains; it is a flower that can grow without light or freedom.

A friend takes someone to their destination when they only asked for directions.

Friendship is both the strongest thing in the world and the most fragile.

Friendship makes strangers disappear.

A friend is someone who sees you the way you want to be.

Friendship is the inevitable result of acknowledging that other people matter.

Sometimes friendship is the wind in our sails and sometimes it is the calm waters.

“Friendship is always a sweet responsibility, never an opportunity.”

KAHLIL GIBRAN

Love is a **sonnet,** but **friendship** can be **anything** from a **limerick** to an **epic poem.**

Memories are the threads that hold the patchwork of friendship together.

Friendship is a **fruit** that is **always** ripe for picking.

A friend is a rare book of which only one copy is made.

Friendship is the art of hooking up to people with no strings attached.

The basis of friendship is simple—trust.

Genuine friends are willing to be there for you; they do not make empty promises.

Friendship speaks softly; it never shouts.

Friendship is an all-terrain vehicle.

"There is a **magnet** in your heart that will **attract** true friends. That magnet is **unselfishness**—thinking of others **first**. When you **learn** to live for others, **they** will live for you."

Paramahansa Yogananda

Friendship is caring deeply about someone and making it obvious.

Friendship is not about agreeing but about debating the differences with humor and respect.

Friendship means never holding on to resentful thoughts.

Friendship is a song that everyone can sing.

Friendship is the clothing of God.

Friendship is a safe place from which to take off or to land.

"If a man does not make new acquaintances as he advances through life, he will soon find himself alone. A man should keep his friendships in constant repair."

SAMUEL JOHNSON

If friendship is the icing on the cake, it's also the cake.

Grapes must grow in sunshine and in rain if you are to enjoy the wine. Friendship is the same.

Friendship is a **game** that everyone **wins** just by **playing.**

Friends can find the common ground, whatever the terrain.

Friendship is a **tool** that must be kept **sharp** if it is to **last** a lifetime.

"True friendship starts by getting to the bottom of yesterday's problems."

CLAUDE ARPI

If you can't decide whether someone is your friend, they probably aren't.

The true value of friendship is in the friendship itself.

Friendship is interdependent independence.

Some people spend their lives flitting about on the surface while their friends swim quietly beneath them.

"In times of prosperity friends will be plenty; in time of adversity not one in twenty."

ENGLISH PROVERB

Friendship is when you hold all the aces and still allow the other person to win the game.

Friendship is a journey to the center of a circle.

Friendship is the **golden chain** by which society is **bound** together.

When you remove suspicion from a relationship, friendship is all that remains.

"Instead of loving your enemies, treat your friends a little better."

EDGAR WATSON HOWE

Friends come and go as leaves fall from a tree: to allow others to grow in their place.

A friendship is **greater** than the **sum** of its **parts**.

Friendship is the fountain of truth.

Friendship means accepting your responsibilities.

If someone offers you their friendship, put down whatever else you are carrying and approach them with open arms.

Friendship gives you the freedom to choose the moments when you wish to be alone.

Friendship seeks out wise companions.

"Friends should be preferred to kings."

VOLTAIRE

Friendship is a rainbow between two hearts.

Friends are not **made;** they are **recognized.**

Friendship is shared silence.

No one ever destroyed a friendship by listening.

To **be** a friend requires **vigilance** of one's thoughts, words, **and** actions.

Friendship should not be approached with pride, fear, or mistrust, for it is a seed that cannot flourish in a barren heart.

Friendship is staying behind to catch up.

Friendship is about knowing when to say "yes" and "no."

There is **no** effective substitute for **having** a friend or for **being** one.

Friendship is a gift that must be given as well as received.

"True friendship is never serene."

Marie de Rabutin-Chantal

Friends give you an invitation to the banquet of life.

The true test of friendship is how far you are prepared to go to keep it.

Friendship **can** be spoken **without** words.

Friendship is discovering fragments of yourself in others.

Friendship is the only game where those with the most to lose walk away with the biggest prize.

Friendship is being prepared for **anything** while expecting **nothing.**

To be a friend you must place your happiness in the hands of others.

Friendship grows wherever the seeds of trust are planted.

Friendship begins at home.

"Friendship is Love without his wings!"

Lord Byron

Friendship is what happens when hearts collide.

Friends are people who **love** the world **through** each other.

Friendship is **giving** someone a **forest** of oak trees when they ask for an **acorn**.

You must spend time carefully gathering wood before you can light a fire. Friendship is the same.

Friendship is a winding mountain path that may not be the quickest way to the summit but guarantees a more comfortable journey.

Friendship lives in our minds but grows through the cracks in our hearts.

Friends are like vitamins: We supplement each other's minimum daily requirements.

Looking for friendship means looking for angels on earth.

Friendship is an **uncut** diamond that must be **shaped** with skill and patience to make it **sparkle**.

Friendship is the difference between breathing and living.

"However rare true love may be, it is less so than true friendship."

François, Duc de La Rochefoucauld

Friendship is a living thing that lasts because it is nourished with kindness, empathy, and understanding.

Friendship is the natural result of following your interests and helping others to follow theirs.

Genuine friendship is a candle that grows bigger the brighter it burns.

Each friend is a prayer answered.

Friendship is to understand and to be understood.

Good friends are the best collectibles.

Friendship is the triumph of the imagination over intelligence.

The bonds that link us together are vital and unique. The name of one of these bonds is friendship.

"Friendship is a sheltering tree."

SAMUEL TAYLOR COLERIDGE

Friendship is one of humankind's most basic needs.

Friendship is the **ability** to **enjoy** the ripples on the surface of a calm lake **without** throwing stones.

Friendship is the answer to life's questions.

Friends are God's way of taking care of us.

Love is blind, but friendship is clairvoyant.

Friendship is an iron chain that never rusts.

"When you ask God for a gift,
Be thankful if He sends,
Not diamonds, pearls, or riches,
But the love of real true friends."

HELEN STEINER RICE

Friendship is the calm before, during, and after the storm.

Friends are the clues God leaves us so that we can find our way back to him.

Friendship is warm rain and cooling winds.

Friendship is the fuel that allows common people to achieve uncommon results.

Trends come and go, but friendship has always been the biggest growth area.

You **cannot** make friends with **someone** you have **never** met, but you **can** prepare yourself for the **moment** when you **will**.

Friendship is like a precious ornament that bounces whenever it is dropped.

Friendship is about growing flowers rather than pressing them.

Problems were invented to give friends a purpose.

Friendship is an unusual physical law that states that positives attract.

Friendship is going it alone together.

Friends are messages of faith.

Friendship is not a spectator sport.

Sometimes a friend is all you have and all you need.

2

Honesty and Trust

"Cultivate solitude and quiet and a few sincere friends, rather than mob merriment, noise, and thousands of nodding acquaintances."

William Powell

I never have to examine your motives.

You **state** the **obvious** when it **needs** to be stated.

Even when you are sure I'll never find out the truth, you won't lie to me.

You would rather hurt me with the truth than mislead me with a lie.

You accept the outcomes of your actions.

You are truthful even when you stand to lose out as a result.

You pay close attention to those things that aren't fighting for your attention.

"Truth springs from argument amongst friends."

DAVID HUME

You return most of the things that you borrow!

When you achieve success you acknowledge those who helped you.

You **recognize** qualities in me that are **invisible** to others—especially to **myself**.

Even if there isn't enough to go around, you don't mind waiting your turn.

You are just the same when nobody is watching.

"If you want an accounting of your worth, count your friends."

MERRY BROWNE

You're not afraid to stand with the minority.

When you do not understand something, you admit it.

You don't care who gets the credit for your achievements.

I cherish the fact that you **choose** your thoughts as **carefully** as your words.

To you, elegance is more important than luxury.

You would never harm others in order to satisfy your view of the world.

Nobody can bully you into silence.

You do not **build** your **emotional** life on the **frailties** of **others.**

Right is **more** important to you than **being** right.

I know you will always put things back where you found them.

You don't use my anxieties as a springboard for talking about yourself.

"Friendship consists in forgetting what one gives, and remembering what one receives."

ALEXANDRE DUMAS THE YOUNGER

You try to understand the things that you fear.

We never argue over unimportant details.

You convert your convictions into your conduct.

You make more of yourself available than most.

When you don't like someone, you try to get to know them better.

I admire your unfailing belief that people's intentions in life are basically good.

You are more concerned with your character than your reputation.

You are prepared to treat everyone with respect, no matter who they are and whether others think they deserve it.

You don't just stick your neck out for a photo finish.

I am in awe of the way you look the world straight in the face.

You announce your goals and disguise your achievements.

You never let your knowledge get in the way of your innocence.

Whenever you get the opportunity to say a kind word, you take it.

"Certain flaws are necessary for the whole. It would seem strange if old friends lacked certain quirks."

JOHANN WOLFGANG VON GOETHE

I would tell you anything, even though you know everything about me already.

At all times, you are gentle with yourself and others.

Whether or not they deserve it, you give people your full attention.

You're **never** so perfect that you **don't** yield to a **little** temptation now and again.

Even when I **know** you're **just** saying something to be kind, I **still** believe what you say!

You judge people from where they are, not from where you are.

When it comes to trust you usually err on the other side of caution.

You command gently and follow with intelligence.

“Friendship without self-interest is one of the rare and beautiful things of life.”

JAMES F. BYRNES

Whatever I have to say, you **never** finish listening **before** I have finished talking.

You recognize the difference between losing your balance and stumbling over the truth.

You refuse to make your mind up about somebody just because they have made their mind up about you.

The beauty in the world unmasks itself to you because you have an open heart.

In an awkward situation, you always try to put others at their ease.

You **believe** that curiosity is **more important** than intelligence.

By refusing to accept anything but the best, you usually get it.

You try to correct your mistakes quickly rather than ignore them.

The advice you offer is always advice that you are prepared to take yourself.

"A friend is someone who sees through you and still enjoys the view."

WILMA ASKINAS

Whenever we disagree, you are always the first to say sorry.

While others are trying to think up excuses, you make promises.

You seem perfectly content with what you already have.

When you **achieve** something amazing, you're **prepared** to **admit** that **luck** played its **part**.

You always do what you say you'll do.

You can **talk** to **anyone** and **really** connect with them.

You demand to be treated with love and respect.

You never let the sun go down on your anger.

You accept yourself without complaint.

I **never** have to ask you **twice**.

With you it's safe to think out loud.

You don't say, "I told you so"— even if you did!

"How often we find ourselves turning our backs on our actual friends, that we may go and meet their ideal cousins."

HENRY DAVID THOREAU

You try to keep your feet on the ground, in case someone needs to lean on you.

When someone treats you unfairly, you don't try to get even.

Being kind is **more** important to you than **being** important.

You look for ways to win that don't involve beating others.

You frequently gain the trust of those around you by defending those who are absent.

"Friends aren't jumper cables. You don't throw them into the trunk and pull them out for emergencies."

Charlie Krueger

When you hug someone, you are never the first to let go.

When **others** are **delighting** in gossip, you **never** get involved.

You are like a tube of toothpaste. You come through in a tight squeeze.

When we **argue**, another gem of **truth** is discovered.

You open your eyes, your heart, your mind, and your mouth—in that order.

When you are given a compliment, you accept it graciously.

You don't believe something just because you have been told it.

"To find a friend one must close one eye— to keep him, two."

NORMAN DOUGLAS

When, despite my best efforts, I put you in the uncomfortable position of forgiver, you always accept the role.

Whether a person can do everything or nothing for you, you treat them the same.

I **welcome** your criticism because I **know** that you have **genuine** confidence in my **abilities**.

You ask a question and then listen to my reply.

When you say "I'm sorry," you always look me in the eye.

You try to do things the best way rather than just your own way.

While I was trying to keep up with the Joneses, you made them your friends and now they are my friends, too.

You give **more** than you take and take **less** than you need.

The only time you ever go behind my back is to pat it.

You seek respect above popularity.

When I think of honesty and integrity I think of you.

You listen to what I say and to what I don't say.

You never resort to gimmicks.

You don't want it all, just your share.

You appreciate beauty for its own sake, not for what you can do with it.

You do not speak because you have all the answers. You speak because you have a voice.

You give me what I deserve, never less.

You never **let** anyone else **set** your standards. You are **always** yourself.

You remind me not to believe everything I know.

When I get on my high horse, you're never too proud to offer me a ride on your donkey!

When you push me too hard, it's easy to tell you to be more gentle.

"Without wearing any mask we are conscious of, we have a special face for each friend."

OLIVER WENDELL HOLMES

3

You Show Me the Way

"Don't walk in front of me, I may not follow; don't walk behind me, I may not lead; walk beside me, and just be my friend."

ALBERT CAMUS

You encourage me to distinguish between sound ideas and ideas that sound good.

I can trust you never to be neutral.

When I'm barking up the wrong tree, you lead me out of the woods.

Thank you for encouraging me to see that life is not a race but a journey.

You are the stone against which I test the mettle of my beliefs.

I've learned to appreciate that happiness comes from within by following your example.

You urge me to break free from routine and follow my dreams.

You think big thoughts and relish small pleasures.

You never use more words than you need.

You offer me **impressions** rather than **opinions**.

If something is **inevitable**, you do **not** waste time **fighting** it.

"Never refuse any advance of friendship, for if nine out of ten bring you nothing, one alone may repay you."

MADAME DE TENCIN

I admire the way you never reject an idea just because you don't know enough about it.

You rate performance over potential.

You are prepared to **stand back** and let others **take their turn** as leaders.

When the window of opportunity appears, you don't allow me to pull down the blinds.

You **enrich** the **quality** of **every day.**

You treat life as a creation rather than a discovery.

You hatch my chickens before I even have time to count them.

While others are kicking back, you kick forward.

You dare to begin and you dare to quit.

We may walk slowly together, but never backward.

Sometimes you say nothing and it's just what I want to hear.

"Nothing makes the earth seem so spacious as to have friends at a distance; they make the latitudes and longitudes."

HENRY DAVID THOREAU

You are cautious and yet courageous.

You look for solutions rather than excuses.

I **wish** I could be **like you** because you always **make** more opportunities than you **find**.

You remind me that I am younger today than I will be tomorrow.

I do not mind the shadows, because I know this means you are shining a light somewhere nearby.

People appreciate the way you say "I will" instead of "I'll try."

Even if you have **already** made them, you allow **me** to make my **own** mistakes.

You think with your own mind and feel with your own heart.

I have learned from you that playing is more important than working.

You do not have a fixed set of beliefs: You're still collecting some.

You don't have to make **grand** gestures to show me you **care.** A phone call says it all.

You show me how to live without the things I do not need.

Your **words** bring me to myself, like a **voice** carried on the wind **calling** a child home.

When you run into an obstacle, you never blame the obstacle.

You take to the open road with lightness of foot and heart and leave it with curiosity.

For you there is no finish line, only another place to start from.

When I go down to the river of your heart, it is never dry.

You remind me that it's never too late to begin.

You adapt yourself cheerfully to new things.

You're never too busy to look me up.

"Sometimes all a person needs is a hand to hold and a heart to understand."

ANDY ROONEY

You listen a **hundred times** before you speak **once**.

Your **securities** far outshine your **insecurities**.

When the writing is on the wall, you knock down the wall.

You never rob me of the opportunity to make a bad choice on my own.

I can rely on you either to find a way or to make one.

You trust nature to give you some of the answers.

The thoughts that escape from my mouth don't seem to bother you.

You help me **recognize** when I **have** choices and when I **don't.**

You're **thrilled** by what's around the **next corner**, but you don't **rush** to **reach** it.

Others cross my path but you make me look at the view.

"But every road is rough to me
That has no friend to cheer it."

ELIZABETH SHANE

You do not **measure** what is **possible** by what has gone **before**.

When I was inconsolable you did not run away from my sadness.

You never look too far ahead nor too far behind.

Not only do you know where you are going, but you know who you will share it with when you arrive.

You never ask a question unless the answer makes a difference.

I can clearly see how much you enjoy simple pleasures.

When necessary, you have the courage to take big steps.

"A single rose can be my **garden** . . . a single friend, my **world**."

LEO BUSCAGLIA

You don't compare yourself with others.

You always adjust your sails to catch the wind.

When I lack the tools, you dig even deeper.

You inspire me to find that something inside myself that is superior to circumstance.

You encourage me to think "What if?"

You urge me to see the sense in the world.

Like the feathers in an arrow, you help me to fly straight.

“The most beautiful discovery true friends make is that they can grow separately without growing apart.”

ELIZABETH FOLEY

At times of darkness, you scatter light.

You strive for excellence instead of perfection.

Instead of waiting for inspiration, you open new frontiers.

When the cards are stacked against me, you reshuffle the deck and deal again.

You paper over my cracks.

The only time you walk away from me is to check if the coast is clear.

I can see more clearly when I climb up on your shoulders.

You always try to help me even when you're not sure how to.

I admire the **way** you view **every** stumbling block as a **stepping**-stone.

It doesn't matter how small my steps are because you keep me heading in the right direction.

"Friendship of the mind sees no destination. Friendship of the heart sees destination everywhere."

SRI CHINMOY

You swim upstream with me when everyone else is going with the flow.

Things develop when you're in the picture.

You've taught me that life doesn't have to be a popularity contest.

Without even trying, you have made a big difference in my life.

All other advice is free, but yours is priceless.

You reach for my hand and touch my heart.

Walking with you in the dark is better than walking alone in the sunshine.

"How rare and wonderful is that flash of a moment when we realize we have discovered a friend."

William E. Rothschild

You square things just by being around!

You have added colors to my life.

When I come unstuck, you stick to me.

You share your friends with me.

When it hurts to look back, and I'm scared to look forward, I suddenly notice you standing beside me.

You hear the song in my heart and sing it to me when I forget the tune.

Friendship is a perfect illustration of how daily miracles appear in the most ordinary of circumstances.

When I need help you never ask if there's anything you can do. You just do it.

You gently nudge me if I'm not paying attention when good things come my way.

"Each friend represents a world in us, a world possibly not born until they arrive, and it is only by this meeting that a new world is born."

ANAÏS NIN

If everyone else in the world walked away I could rely on you to stay.

You are there for me even when you would prefer to be somewhere else.

You show me the way to turn my mind and body into instruments of freedom.

Friendship is a priceless treasure, never to be bought or sold—it can only be cherished.

I know that you would be willing to give me what I hope I will never have to ask for.

If I **refuse** your support, you are **proud** that I can do it on my **own.**

Even when you don't have all the answers, you ask me the right questions.

When I lose my way, you are the beacon that guides me home.

"Love is only chatter; friends are all that matter."

Frank Gelett Burgess

When I stumble, you pick me up, dust me off, and get me moving again.

You help me to free myself from my opinions, so I can consider the opinions of others.

You always find time for me when I can't find time for myself.

It's a jungle out there. Thank you for being my survival kit.

You let me shelter under your wings while I grow my own.

When my spirits are low, you show me something to be thankful for.

You help me to face the unknown, because you have allowed me to see your own fear so that I know I am not alone.

"Friends are people you make a **part** of your life **just** because you **feel** like it. Basically your friends are **not** your friends for any particular **reason**. They are your friends for **no** particular reason."

FREDERICK BUECHNER

The only time you ever get in my way is to stop me from falling.

You made sacrifices so that I could follow my dreams.

When everyone else was jumping on the bandwagon, you offered me a piggyback. Thanks for the ride!

When everyone else is thinking only of themselves, you think of me.

You are my safety net when I fall off life's trapeze.

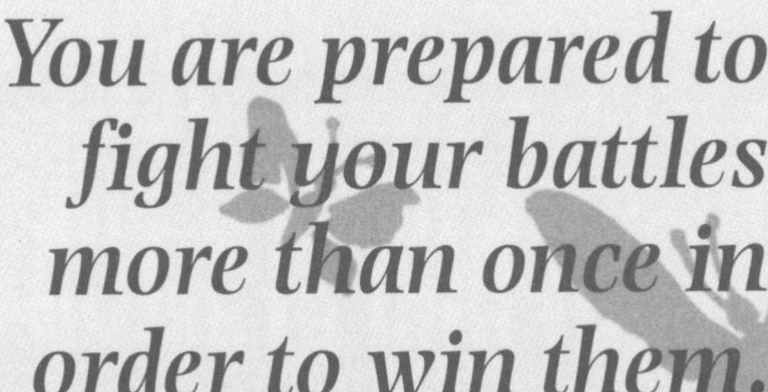

You are prepared to fight your battles more than once in order to win them.

You're the whole nine yards and you'd jump them for me, too.

When you say "I'll catch you later," I know that you probably will.

You help me trust my ability to handle whatever comes my way.

Whenever I take a wrong turn, you always wait for me while I retrace my steps.

"Treat your friends as you do your pictures and place them in their best light."

JENNIE JEROME CHURCHILL

The walls that I build around myself are no obstacles to you. You always find a way to scale them.

When the world is too busy, you help to slow me down.

I am most sure of you on those occasions when I am most unsure of myself.

You are willing to upset the apple cart to find the fruit of compassion.

Instead of waiting for your boat to come in, you swim out to it.

You **share** your **knowledge** and **wisdom** with me, **knowing** that you will **not** be **diminished** when these gifts make me **fly**.

You Know Me

You can pick the lock to my thoughts.

You never deny my right to grow and seek the truth.

We can make small talk without mentioning the weather.

"Never judge someone by who he's in love with; judge him by his friends. People fall in love with the most appalling people. Take a cool, appraising glance at his pals."

CYNTHIA HEIMEL

The **only** time you let me down is when I'm **too** puffed up.

You notice things in me that no one has looked quite far enough to see before.

You love me for my sake, not for your own.

I like having you around when I feel like being myself.

We don't always think the same but we always think together.

When you see people dancing you try to hear their music.

"No distance of place or lapse of time can lessen the friendship of those who are thoroughly persuaded of each other's worth."

ROBERT SOUTHEY

You make me feel important and you do it sincerely.

I may **wear** a thousand **masks** but you **always** recognize that it's **me** underneath.

You can put a finger on my faults without rubbing them in.

Thanks to you, I have learned that no one is immune from life.

Even if I fail, you admire me for attempting great things.

You **never** assume that the way you **see** things is the way things **are**.

You give me the confidence to change because you accept me just the way I am.

You never refuse my homemade cakes.

I must have done something really great to deserve you!

You understand yourself in order to understand others.

"Friendship with oneself is all-important because without it one cannot be friends with anybody else in the world."

ELEANOR ROOSEVELT

We honor our differences and enjoy our similarities.

You expect a great deal from me but never ask it.

Instead of moving me around to get a better picture, you tune in to my wavelength.

You do not consider that others are lost just because they happen to choose a different route from you.

I know that you will always see me through your own eyes rather than other people's.

You help me to write my worries on the sand so that they can be carried away by the tide.

My **boredom** has been **cured** by your **curiosity**.

You open my eyes to my own greatness.

I know **YOU** better than I know **myself**.

When you have **nothing** to **say**, you say **nothing**.

When my dreams turn to dust, you don't complain about the mess.

You encourage me to consider all the options.

"Perhaps the most delightful friendships are those in which there is much agreement, much disputation, and yet more personal liking."

George Eliot

Before making yourself understood, you try to understand others.

You have brought me contentment in place of the victory that I used to seek.

When words fail me, yours come in very handy.

You **know** what it's like because **you** have been **there** with **me.**

Where others see copper, you see gold in me.

Whether I act upon or ignore your advice, your reaction is always the same.

Even when I am fooling everyone else, you can see the truth and the hurt in me.

Where others can see black and white, you see all the shades of gray.

You accept my limitations and push my limits.

"A **true** friend will **see** you through when others **see** that you **are** through."

LAURENCE J. PETER

Sometimes the best advice you give me is listening.

You have shown me that I'm never too old to dream new dreams.

You **try** to be the **sort** of friend to me that **you** would **like** to **have.**

When I am feeling **bristly**, you **never** give me the **brush-off**.

You don't need an explanation for everything.

You neither look down on me nor keep up with me.

"I have friends in overalls whose friendship I would not swap for the favor of the kings of the world."

THOMAS A. EDISON

I can always rely on you to know how I feel even before I speak.

You don't finish my sentences, but you could.

It's easy to be me with you.

If I want some time alone, you don't get mad.

I can reveal my weaknesses to you.

We may not be two peas in a pod, but it is our differences that keep our friendship fun.

You believe I'm more special than even I think I am, but you'll tell me when I'm being a fool.

You know your own faults well enough to forgive me mine.

You help me to put the past behind me, but you understand when I need to say good-bye to it in my own time.

You can easily sense the needs and feelings of others.

I don't have to tidy the house before you come round.

"Never injure a friend, even in jest."

MARCUS TULLIUS CICERO

You always have the courage to tell me what I need to hear.

When I blot my copybook, you tear out the page and burn it to keep us warm.

We have nothing to prove to one another.

You know all my faults and still you manage to like me.

"A friend may well be reckoned the masterpiece of Nature."

RALPH WALDO EMERSON

I can make a fool of myself and you'll still be my friend.

I am in awe of your ability to watch the unseen and listen to the unheard.

You help me to think of myself as becoming the person I want to be.

You patiently tolerate all my questions.

"What is a friend? A single soul dwelling in two bodies."

ARISTOTLE

Like a mirror, you reflect my strengths and swallow my weaknesses.

You wish me well for my own sake and without envy.

We can disagree and still stay friends.

I am **amazed** that you can **always** put up with my **bad moods.**

The joy of my presence is all you want from me.

Thank you for giving me the freedom to be imperfect.

You always put friendship first.

"Keep a fair-sized **cemetery** in your backyard, in which to **bury** the faults of your friends."

HENRY WARD BEECHER

Before I met you I didn't know what I wanted and I was hurting myself to get it.

It's **fantastic** to know, with **absolute** confidence, that **someone** cares.

You understand my past, believe in my future, and accept me today just the way I am.

You understand the stupid things about me.

Although you are an important part of my life, you don't try to run it.

You accept the differences in others and you don't try to change them.

You **believe** in me even when I **don't** believe in myself. You **trust** me even when I do **not** trust myself. You **give** me hope even when I think I am **beyond** it.

You see more potential in me than I see in myself.

"Friends are not the people you meet at the top; they are the people who were with you at the bottom."

MICHAEL MARINO

Without **asking** for **evidence**, you are **able** to **believe**.

You tolerate my inhibitions and help me to overcome them.

I don't have to act bubbly with you when I'm feeling flat.

I can trust you to tell me things I don't want to tell myself.

Extraordinary things happen when you are around.

When I've cooked my goose, you talk turkey.

"Two persons cannot long be friends if they cannot forgive each other's little failings."

JEAN DE LA BRUYÈRE

You are **more** interested in who I **am** than in who I am **expected** to be.

I know you would never belittle my ambitions or laugh at my dreams.

You help me both to forget myself and to remember who I am.

You challenge me more than anyone I know.

I can **always** trust you **not** to make assumptions **about** me.

You **live** your **beliefs** but you never **force** them on others, and **still** they **follow** the **example** you set.

When I am hiding you come looking for me.

"We know our friends by their defects rather than by their merits."

W. Somerset Maugham

You always give me your approval, even though you are the one person from whom I do not feel the need to seek it.

Even when you **know** that I am **utterly** wrong, you **stick up** for me.

"Let us be grateful
to people who
make us happy;
they are the
charming gardeners
who make our souls
blossom."

MARCEL PROUST

5

I Need You

One kind word from you can warm a week in winter.

"Some people go to priests; others to poetry; I to my friends."

VIRGINIA WOOLF

Thanks for being here when everyone else was over there.

**I used to run
through life so fast
I only saw my goals,**

**Until you made me
see that God loves
all human souls.**

When all's said and done, you've usually done more than you've said.

You always give me a lift home even if it's out of your way.

When others bottle it, your support is always on tap.

You're never far at all when I have a close call.

You have **taught** me to **face** my problems **one** at a **time.**

You are my landing lights.

The things that you do take me up a peg or two.

"Friends are born, not made."

HENRY ADAMS

When life hits me below the belt, you help me to get my breath back.

You **believe** that **even** the **point** of **no return** can be a **turning point.**

When the chips are down, you always send out for pizza.

We don't just hang out; we hang together.

You have your say and then you stay.

In times of **trouble**, when others bring me formal **gifts** and **flowers**, you bring me a **wink** and a **smile**.

When I am having a difficult journey, talking to you helps me to forget how sore my feet are.

"I have **three** chairs in my house: **one** for solitude, **two** for friendship, **three** for company."

HENRY DAVID THOREAU

The guest book in my heart shows that you have made the most visits.

In a difficult situation you are often the first to drop your barriers in order to find a way through.

**I do not love you
by what the world
says friendship is;
I love you only by what
I know friendship is.**

When I'm **stuck**, you **help** me to **see** the **next** step.

Even when you know I cannot repay you, you lend me your support.

You dispense practical advice, not friendly platitudes.

You remind me that there is always enough to go round.

I have strength inside of me now, thanks to you.

When I'm driving myself up the wall, you help me down.

You turn a vicious circle into a carousel.

Friends come and go. Thanks for coming.

You are my eyes when I'm too scared to open mine.

"Don't be dismayed at good-byes. A farewell is necessary before you can meet again. And meeting again, after moments or lifetimes, is certain for those who are friends."

RICHARD BACH

Friends always try to meet in the middle, but you seem to reach me first.

When you reach the summit, the first thing you do is look down and reach for my hand.

You give much when you have much to give and when you have little to give.

You support me in my first beginnings to help me reach my undiscovered ends.

"A friend is one who incessantly pays us the compliment of expecting from us all the virtues, and who can appreciate them in us."

HENRY DAVID THOREAU

You remind me that life is great the way it is now.

When the going gets tough you are more than enough.

You are aware of the treasure of an ordinary day.

For you, success and failure are never final.

I don't know **how** you do it; I'm just **glad** that you **do.**

Some people help me to **find** my gifts; you help me to **share** them.

You remind me that nothing is more important than this day.

"Hold a true friend with both your hands."

NIGERIAN PROVERB

I know that you need me as much as I need you.

I can rely on you to keep your head in a crisis.

An apology comes quickly from your heart.

You don't try to solve problems that aren't yours to solve.

You help me pick up the pieces of shattered dreams.

If you **need** my help, you're **never** too proud to **ask** for it.

“The world is round so that friendship may encircle it.”

PIERRE TEILHARD DE CHARDIN

Loneliness doesn’t get a look in when you’re looking out for me.

You can lift even the heaviest of hearts.

Without you everything in my life would seem smaller—except my phone bill.

You think actively and act thoughtfully.

The climb is less severe if you are near.

"A true friend is the greatest of all blessings."

François, Duc de La Rochefoucauld

I know I can always turn to you when I've popped all my bubble wrap.

You are more interested in promoting goodwill than in being successful.

I like the way you stop and think.

A friend fills a place that was left open.

You're far out and close by at the same time.

You don't mind driving me to the airport.

When I give you a thousand reasons why I can't, you give me the one reason why I can.

You look for optimal solutions, not perfect ones.

I know that you would never give up on anybody.

When we are chatting on-line, you don't mind that I'm a slow typist.

When you leave I miss the noise.

When I'm feeling unbalanced you tip the scales of life in my favor.

Although we may disagree, we never have to start all over again.

If I could have one of your qualities it would be your enthusiasm.

You **search** for that **something extra** that can **improve** things.

You know **when** to **stand up** and **speak** and **when** to **sit down** and **listen**.

The **only** time you put me **down** is when you're **too tired** to carry me anymore.

I hope one day you can lean on me as much as I have leaned on you.

You never let me hang up in despair.

"Friendship ought to be a gratuitous joy, like the joys afforded by art, or life."

SIMONE WEIL

I need **you** to remind **me** that sometimes I'm **ahead**, sometimes I'm **behind**.

You always manage to turn a loss into a new discovery.

You know when to hug me and tell me that it's going to be okay.

When I talk to you I hear the word "could" instead of "must" and "should."

"The meeting of two personalities is like the contact of two chemical substances; if there is any reaction, both are transformed."

CARL JUNG

When I am at my lowest ebb, you help me to turn the tide.

You instinctively know what I miss and what I long for.

I treasure all of the little things you do for me without needing a reason.

Your eyes are calm and your mind is peaceful.

"Stay is a charming word in a friend's vocabulary."

LOUISA MAY ALCOTT

You are led by your values, not your circumstances.

You replace "maybe tomorrow" with "here I am."

I know you will always have chocolate.

It's not that I can't live without you; it's just that I don't want to.

You always leave a light on in your heart.

"It is not so much our friends' help that helps us as the confident knowledge that they will help us."

EPICURUS

You tolerate everything except intolerance.

Wherever we go we take a little of each other with us.

Even **though** we both **change**, our friendship **stays** the **same**.

Our friendship **doesn't** make the world go **round**, but it makes the **ride** **worthwhile.**

If I ask for time alone, you always know exactly when to come back.

I rely on you to show me who I am and where I want to go.

If I were to plant a seed every time I think of you, I could walk forever in a sea of green.

"My friends have made the story of my life. In a thousand ways they have turned my limitations into beautiful privileges, and enabled me to walk serene and happy in the shadow cast by my deprivation."

HELEN KELLER

You force me to clear out my clutter.

When I won't budge, you give me a gentle nudge.

You always look before I leap.

Even when we are walking in opposite directions we remain side by side.

Rather than pretending you know them already, you set out to find the answers.

Your loyalty asks for no reward but that our friendship should continue to grow.

Some people live in a dream world and others face reality, but with your help we can turn one into the other.

You always reply to my e-mails.

You're all talk—pep talk.

"The best time to make friends is before you need them."

ETHEL BARRYMORE

You help me to listen to my inner voice.

With you beside me I am willing to explore life outside my comfort zone.

When my heart has been broken, you teach me to trust again.

First you **grabbed** my **attention**, and then you **shared** some of your most **precious** secrets.

You **surprise** me with **little** sweet acts of **kindness.**

"No man can be happy without a friend, nor be sure of his friend till he is unhappy."

THOMAS FULLER

You have **many** interests; **some** of them have **now** become **my** passions.

You blow the winds of change in my direction.
You always share your happiness with me.

When I need to blow off some steam you're my safety valve.

You never have to pencil me in.

I never have to mind my p's and q's, just *U* and *I*.

You help me to become the person I couldn't be without you.

We are cut from the same cloth, you and me; that's why you can patch me up.

I am not **afraid** of **storms** when we **sail** our **ship** together.

You allow me the freedom to change because you have watched me changing and growing for so long.

You help me transform loneliness into solitude.

"Friendship is the first and basic human conviction."

DR. WILLIAM S. SADLER

What you have you give, instead of wishing you had more to give.

The circle of your compassion grows wider every day.

You protect me with your prayers, magnify me with your love, and refresh me with your laughter.

"If you have **one** true friend you have **more** than your share."

THOMAS FULLER

You give me sixty minutes in my hour of need.

I can always rely on you to go out of your way to make another's day.

I can always depend on you to depend on me.

On life's journey I often turn around and congratulate myself **on the path** I have taken. But when I look back at our friendship, though the **winds of time** have erased our steps, I am reminded that together we have created something more important than **mere footprints**.

6

Laughter and Tears

"In the sweetness of friendship let there be laughter, for in the dew of little things the heart finds its morning and is refreshed."

JAMES ALLEN

We've shared many smiles and many tears, but nothing beats the laughter.

You're absolutely determined to enjoy whatever you are doing.

I can phone you when I have nothing to say.

When you see me without a smile, you give me one of yours.

You **entertain** me rather than try to **improve** me and **usually** end up doing **both.**

Some people grab life by the throat; you tickle it under the chin.

There's **nothing** as **much** fun as doing **nothing** **much** with you.

You focus on what you have rather than what you have lost.

"It seems to me that trying to live without friends is like milking a bear to get cream for your coffee. It is a whole lot of trouble, and then not worth much after you get it."

ZORA NEALE HURSTON

Whenever you are on thin ice, you start to dance.

You take each day and make it better.

You take big bites out of your slice of life.

You have the courage to make a fool of yourself.

Even when we don't know where we're heading, we end up laughing somewhere.

You recognize that your body can be a dance hall as well as a temple.

I love the way you wave at children on school buses.

You second my emotions and lighten the load.

You are **generous** to **yourself** as well as to **others.**

The only thing you don't care about is who you smile at.

You are mature enough to revel in moments of immaturity.

Your eyes shine with sparkling contradictions.

We may **make** mistakes **together**, but it's **fun** all the **same.**

When I ask you a dumb question I can rely on you to give me a dumb answer.

You're charming, witty, good-looking, and intelligent. We're so alike!

"We are not friends for the laughs we spend, but the tears we save."

NIKKI GIOVANNI

Friends turn a **meal** into a **feast** and a **house** into a **home.**

You're silly at the right moments.

You've got your head screwed on, even though you are a little twisted!

Embarrassing me in front of my parents—just one more service you offer!

You **encourage** me to take things **less seriously**; after all, they're **only** things.

You try to mix a little foolishness in with your serious plans.

I admire your perseverance.

You make every day a friendship day.

Whenever I'm at a **loose end**, I know that you won't be too **tied up** to talk.

"We cherish our friends not for their ability to amuse us, but for our ability to amuse them."

EVELYN WAUGH

In the most formal of situations, you manage to remain appropriately informal.

I ate all the chocolate and you forgave me.

Everything that happens in your life you try to love, and you laugh at anything you can't.

Your **intelligence** and **wisdom** are demonstrated by your continued **cheerfulness**.

By never trying to be noticed you never quite manage to be ignored.

I cherish your ability to make your own happiness.

"The greatest healing therapy is friendship and love."

HUBERT H. HUMPHREY

You laugh at my jokes even when they are not very funny and listen to my problems even when they are not very serious.

You treat me like one of the family, but I forgive you!

You set out to do something silly every day.

You **dare** me to be **myself** and then have a good **laugh** at my **insanity**!

If I had a dollar for every time you've helped me out, I could pay back that money you lent me!

You never let other people's laughter shape your experiences.

Friends like you can't be bought—but they can be bribed with ice cream!

What a sense of humor!
It's just like mine!

You cook with reckless abandon.

"The greatest sweetener of human life is Friendship."

JOSEPH ADDISON

You are never SO busy questioning things that you can't laugh at them.

Whenever I feel crumpled you straighten me out.

You seriously believe that nothing should be taken too seriously.

While others judge me by what I have already done, you remind me of what I am capable of doing.

Your laugh can turn a fiasco into a fiesta.

"We are friends and I do like to pass the day with you in serious and inconsequential chatter."

JEANETTE WINTERSON

The door to your heart is always open.

Our jokes just keep on coming.

You'll listen to my music.

You are worth your weight in chocolate chip cookies!

When I borrow your car, you never stand in my way.

You're mellow, like a good bottle of wine, and fun when you're uncorked!

I can always depend on you to double my joy and halve my sorrow.

"The language of friendship is not words but meanings."

HENRY DAVID THOREAU

When we are together we cry with laughter at things that aren't even funny.

You dance with me in the sunlight and walk with me in the shadows.

*If I could reach up
and hold a star for every
time you made me laugh,
the entire evening sky
would be in the palm
of my hand.*

**We are tied together by
memories, tears, laughter,
and smiles.**

"Thy friendship oft has made my heart to ache; Do be my enemy— for friendship's sake."

WILLIAM BLAKE

You are the **happiest** person I **know** because you **don't** try to be **happier** than everyone else.

There is nothing I wouldn't do for you, and there is nothing you wouldn't do for me.

How can I be sad? You look so silly when you try to cheer me up!

You sympathize with my strength, not my weakness.

Whenever life becomes bizarre, I look for you and there you are.

When my **heart** has been **broken** and all my **hopes** have run **away**, you **mend** it and then **fill** it up again with **laughter**.

Your sense of fun is a horizon that expands every time I approach it.

You listen to my heart.

You're different, and I'd really miss you if you weren't there.

You have frequent attacks of smiling.

You're not embarrassed when I make a fool of myself.

We can make harmless fun of each other.

"It is a sweet thing,
friendship, a dear balm,
A happy and auspicious
bird of calm . . ."

PERCY BYSSHE SHELLEY

You ignite the spark of humor in every situation.

You encourage me to hit the high notes.

"Friendship is certainly the finest balm for the pangs of disappointed love."

JANE AUSTEN

When I suffered a great loss you didn't know what to say, but instead of walking away, you simply helped me to cry.

When I struggle you give me a huggle.

Whenever I ask "Why did this happen to me?" you remind me to ask the same of all the joy that comes my way.

You **keep** me **young** even though you **never** stop **reminding** me about how **old** I am **getting!**

"Sometimes our light goes out but is blown into flame by another human being. Each of us owes deepest thanks to those who have rekindled this light."

ALBERT SCHWEITZER

When all the trees were bare, you spoke of the future when we would pick the fruit together.

You often laugh at yourself and invite others to join in.

Our shared laughter makes my head reel with exuberance.

Whenever my life is going through a dry spell, you point out the high-water mark.

You never feel sorry for yourself.

"When people care for you and cry for you, they can straighten out your soul."

LANGSTON HUGHES

If **listening** is an **art**, you have a **natural talent** for it.

My heart dances because of you.

You fly because you take yourself lightly.

When it's time to face the music, you help me to play a different tune.

"Have no friends not equal to yourself."

CONFUCIUS

7

You Inspire Me

"My friend, if I could give you one thing, I would wish for you the ability to see yourself as others see you. Then you would realize what a truly special person you are."

B. A. Billingsly

You've taught me it's never too late to start again.

You are comfortable with success.

The breadth of your gifts is matched only by the depth of your soul.

To be a better friend
it's plain to see,
I must be more like you
and less like me.

When my
imagination feels
cooped up, you
give it free rein.

However bad things get, you always have faith that they will get better.

You have a uniqueness that makes people look and pay more attention.

You don't just make impressions; you leave them, too.

"You can make more friends in two months by becoming interested in other people than you can in two years by trying to get other people interested in you."

DALE CARNEGIE

When life isn't offering a game worth playing, you invent a new one.

When you have to jump through hoops just to get through the day, you still seem to have lots of energy left over.

While others ponder, you ask, ask, ask.

You **don't** allow the **unknown** to **affect** you.

In the University of Life you earn top honors.

"If you are successful, you may win false friends and true enemies. Succeed anyway."

MOTHER TERESA

When I'm broken down, you show me your soul.

I admire your self-discipline.

You gain the respect of intelligent and sensitive people.

Instead of waiting for other people to be friendly, you show them how.

Rather than saving it for later, you spend your life now.

To you the present is a gift.

You are not unpredictable; neither are you predictable.

You pay for your wonderful gifts by using them.

“You never lose by loving. You always lose by holding back.”

BARBARA DEANGELIS

You go with the flow, but you're not afraid to cause a stir.

I admire your ability to enjoy your own company.

You draw joy toward you without even realizing you're doing it.

You do not seek happiness but euphoria.

What you can give is more important to you than what you can get.

You have a clear idea of what you want to achieve.

You admire rather than envy.

Win or lose, you do it with grace and humor.

You keep **reaching out** for things that are just **beyond** your **reach.**

Whenever you receive applause, you look genuinely surprised.

You don't count on anybody else to relieve your stress.

"Everyone has a gift for something, even if it is the gift of being a good friend."

MARIAN ANDERSON

When seeking **different** results you **change** your behavior **first.**

When others can only dream, you take action.

You **maximize** your **potential** by **sharing** it with **others.**

I try to follow your example by never taking anything for granted.

You don't blame your parents but instead thank them for having you.

I am **inspired** to write words in **praise** of you.

"When a friend speaks to me, whatever he says is interesting."

JEAN RENOIR

Until you've given everything, you won't give up.

You don't worry about knowing people; you just make yourself worth knowing.

You do not allow your doubts to discourage you.

The fact that you can't do everything doesn't seem to stop you from trying anything.

Even when you only have a few of the pieces, you try to make pictures.

Most of the high spots in my life have come about through your encouragement.

Every day you challenge me to be happy.

You are never boring.

"Though friendship is not quick to burn, it is explosive stuff."

May Sarton

You insist on making your contribution to the world.

Once you have found your peace, you pass it on.

You empower others with the strength of your beliefs.

I'm sure you change the world by your example.

You **bite** off **more** than you can **chew** and **then** you **chew** it.

Whatever the **burden**, you exhibit **grace** under **pressure**.

You're my sixth sense.

You're the skip in my step.

You're the coins in my fountain.

You are my dream catcher.

"A friend is someone who, upon seeing another friend in immense pain, would rather be the one experiencing the pain than watch their friend suffer."

AMANDA GIER

To you, change is more crucial than results.

Your presence is a present to the world.

However little you have, you are still generous with your time.

Sometimes you make me feel irreplaceable.

I find your enthusiasm **contagious**; you could start an **epidemic**.

Every day of your life you scatter creative seeds.

When others can't see the target, you aim straight for the center.

You don't wait for other people's permission to live your life.

You **luxuriate** in the **space between** where you **are** and where you **want to be**.

"My friend is that one whom I can associate with my choicest thought."

Henry David Thoreau

You never let yesterday's disappointments overshadow tomorrow's dreams.

Life is **tough**, but you're **tougher**.

You color outside the lines.

You don't get hung up on the little things.

You **accept** insults graciously, by **ignoring** them.

You **find** the good in **everything**, because you **look** for it.

When the world is going bananas you don't go ape.

If you have something you **don't** need, you give it to someone who **does.**

"One loyal friend is worth ten thousand relatives."

EURIPIDES

Every day, you seek to expand your freedom a little bit more.

Although you believe in miracles, you don't depend on them.

You do so much for so many people who never realize it.

Although you ask for a lot, you take what is offered.

My friend, you light up my life every single day.

You never confuse a single defeat with an ultimate defeat.

You have confidence in the truth, although you may not always be able to comprehend it.

You are prepared to say no to many things to leave you free to say yes at the most important moments.

I'm the first person you call if you've got a good idea.

It's impossible for you to hide your beautiful soul.

You act and leave the talking to the others.

"A friend is a present you give to yourself."

Robert Louis Stevenson

You live your life as if everything is a miracle, and you encourage me to see beauty in the world.

You **open** your arms to **change**, but you **never** let go of your **values**.

Being in your company elevates me.

Because of you, I **believe** there **really** is **good** in the world.

I admire the light that's inside of you.

When I am reaching for the stars, you remind me of the flowers at my feet.

You **help me** to **pursue** what I **want** rather than **settle** for what is **comfortable.**

You never try to stop the rain by complaining.

"Plant a seed of friendship; reap a bouquet of happiness."

LOIS L. KAUFMAN

You never seem to waste energy by worrying.

If it is for the benefit of others, you're not afraid to break the rules.

You never assume that your beliefs and expectations are shared by everybody else.

I've **learned** from **you** to do **ordinary** things in an **extraordinary** way.

You are charming, but you don't rely on it.

Whatever people expect, you always give more.

The only person you try to outstrip is yourself.

I admire your ingenuity.

You rise above the mediocrity of your surroundings.

You believe in a world of peace and you try to spread it wherever you go.

Friendship gives me the courage to lose sight of the shore in my search for new lands.

“Without friends no one would choose to live.”

Aristotle

You do your best and then wait patiently for the results.

Before you think, you always dream a little.

You always try to make a difference.

To you everything is a worthwhile experience.

You're a realist who believes in miracles.

Each day you try to learn something new.

You live your life hoping to find adventure while others secretly hope that they won't.

You are the pearl that has taught me that all the world is my oyster.

How do you manage to be in the midst of trouble and still be calm in your heart?

Your energy is boundless, your honesty is unwavering, and your faith in me is indestructible.

"Every gift from a friend is a wish for your happiness."

Richard Bach

Yesterday's defeats never cause you to complain.

You are the most necessary person I know.

You are motivated by your loves and not your hates.

Like a **rainbow**, you **brighten** my **life** when I have been **through** a **storm**.

Sometimes you hold my hand, but you always hold my attention.

You take pleasure in the simplest things— even me!

Whatever I should do, you make sure I do it.

Your imagination guides you.

You act spontaneously rather than on your fears.

If you were a flower, you'd be a forget-me-not.

You take the cake—and work out the recipe later.

Regardless of the circumstances, you do what needs to be done.

When in doubt you're an optimist.

You have the curiosity of a child.

You take time to wonder.

I didn't think orange went with purple until you showed me a sunset.

8

Friends Are Forever

“Friends are like melons.
Shall I tell you why?
To find one good
you must a hundred try.”

CLAUDE MERMET

It's **you** and **me** against the **world**, so this is your **last** chance to **switch** teams.

There are **acquaintances**, **friends**, and **best friends**—and **then** there is **you**.

You hold your head high, but always at a friendly level.

You're my lead violin.

Without you where would I begin?

You remind me of someone I see when I stare into a calm lake.

You are my endless sky.

I know you choose your friends carefully—thanks for choosing me.

It has taken a short time to know you, but it would take me a lifetime to forget.

"A brother may not be a friend, but a friend will always be a brother."

SAMUEL RICHARDSON

You are my dream team of one.

Our friendship is going to be the stuff of legends.

You are **always** worth the **trouble** and I **know** you'll **never** give up on me.

If I had to live my life again, I'd like to meet you sooner.

With your score, the best of the rest don't pass the friendship test.

You are someone I hope to stay young with while I grow old.

Most things cease to be wonderful when you get used to them, but our friendship just keeps getting better.

We may not always see eye to eye, but we never stop looking.

I'm having the time of your life.

Nobody will ever build a statue dedicated to you, but the music of your life will play on in the hearts of your friends.

"Good company in a journey makes the way seem shorter."

Izaak Walton

You **play** the friendship **game** for **keeps**.

You planted a tree on my birthday.

Right now we are **making** some **great** memories **together**.

I know the future will be a better place if you are there.

A musician must compose music; a poet must write poems; you must make friends.

You are my place in the sun.

The future can wait, so long as we're together.

You leave the best bits for me.

"Then come the wild weather, come sleet or come snow,
We will stand by each other, however it blow."

SIMON DACH

Chance made us **meet;**
time made us **friends.**

You last longer than the tough times.

We are made from the **same mold**, just filled with **different stuff.**

Instead of looking for friends who are like me, now I look for friends who are like you.

Thank you for **never** bragging about your **success** or your **plans**.

You **make up** for some of the **qualities** that I feel I **lack**—but **don't** ask me **which ones**!

When **times** are **hard**, you **keep** your **heart soft**.

You can still remember my favorite poem.

When something matters to me, it matters to you, too.

You recognize that words last longer than temples.

Our friendship is like freshly fallen snow. It bestows an extraordinary kind of silent beauty on ordinary things.

Time spent with you is never long enough.

If friends were flowers, I'd still pick you.

You are like a movie I can watch over and over.

"The ornament of a house is the friends who frequent it."

RALPH WALDO EMERSON

It's **not** that we **disagree**; it's **how** we **disagree** that **makes** us **last**.

You **show** up, **stand** up, **open** up, **put** up, and **make** up with me.

I think I have finally found my place in this world—next to you.

Friendship is not **something** you **seek**, it is **something** you **build.**

If life is a dream, then I'm really glad you're in mine.

Life may be an illusion, but you seem pretty real to me.

We are **all** given **gifts**, but it **looks** like you've **opened** yours **first.**

On the road of life, you're by far the best diversion.

"Never shall I forget the times I spent with you; continue to be my friend, as you will always find me yours."

LUDWIG VAN BEETHOVEN

I don't mind going nowhere as long as you're with me.

Our friendship isn't a big thing; it's a million little things.

You are the best sort of life insurance.

I've never **quite** lost the **wonder** of the **companionship** that you **deliver.**

You'll still be here when I'm past my prime.

"Do not protect yourself by a fence, but rather by your friends."

CZECH PROVERB

We have so much in common, it's almost scary!

I will never forget the memories we have made, and I can't wait for the ones still to come.

We may have our differences, but we always end up on top.

“Similarities create friendships while differences hold them together.”

Anon

The only time you get on my case is to help me pack.

We're never so far out of range that we can't shoot the breeze.

You're a foul-weather friend.

I stop hurrying when I'm with you.

"Truly great friends are hard to find, difficult to leave, and impossible to forget."

G. Randolf

You'll walk miles with me on the beach.

You remember my birthday and forget my age!

You'll always be my friend: You know too much!

Did you know that we share some of my fondest memories?

"Friendship is a meandering river whose course can never be diverted and whose current should not be hastened."

MARGARET POWELL

Every day you make it your job to be my friend. I hope you never retire!

You are like an old comfy chair that I never want to part with.

"My father always used to say that when you die, if you've got five real friends, then you've had a great life."

LEE IACOCCA

We're two of a kind.

You are better than a pair of gloves, because I do not have to drag you around with me for you to keep me warm.

Our friendship will never die—just get reorganized.

When you phone you just have to say "Hi" and I know it's you.

You are worth living for.

It is always hard to say good-bye, but let's never say farewell.

It is your tiny, everyday gifts that are so special: a kind word, a smile, the smallest act of caring.

Even though we **might** spend a **long** time apart, when we come **together** again there is **no** awkwardness.

You're the only person I know who comes with a lifetime guarantee.

When we are long in the tooth we'll sit together and remember our youth.

"When we are young, friends are, like everything else, a matter of course. In the old days we know what it means to have them."

EDVARD HAGERUP GRIEG

You never ask "What's in it for me?"

Forgiveness is just one of your habits.

Wherever you go, you go with all my heart.

Choose to be alone or choose instead to spend your time with friends. Time will pass regardless.

In life you're interested in the whole story, not just your own scenes.

You help me to understand my past and shape my future.

Every year, even though the leaves fall from the trees and the winter storms bring icy winds, I can always warm my heart in front of yours.

You are as dear to me as my own fingers—when things get too difficult, I can always count on you.

When **tomorrow** starts **without** you, you'll **always** be in my thoughts and your **memory** will live on in my **heart**.

We **laugh** so much **together** that when we get **old** we can be sure our **wrinkles** will be in the **right** places.

"Treat your friend as a spectacle."

RALPH WALDO EMERSON

The thought of all the yesterdays we have shared makes me look forward to all the tomorrows we will share and reminds me to make the most of every special day we spend together.

When everyone else was kissing my feet, you gently held my hand.

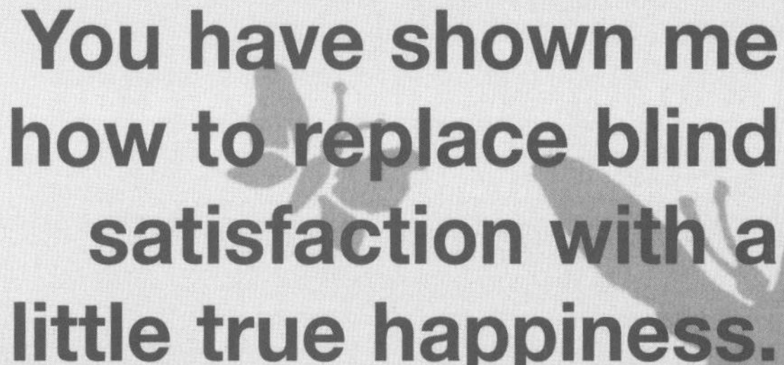

You have shown me how to replace blind satisfaction with a little true happiness.

You are there through ups and downs, smiles and frowns.

If I could change the past, I would change many things, but you would play exactly the same part.

"With clothes the new are best; with friends the old are best."

CHINESE PROVERB

Thanks for letting me be more human.

We will be friends until forever, just you watch.

You will seek me out even in heaven.

You're open all hours.

"True friendship is like sound health; the value of it is seldom known until it be lost."

CHARLES CALEB COLTON

I may **not** remember **exactly** what you **did** or what you **said**, but I will **always** remember **how** you made me **feel**.

Friendship exists for the deepening of the spirit.

Even when we don't talk, your heart still listens.

Even when I try to push you away, you keep coming back.

We have infinite faith
in one another.

A friend gives help and comfort before advice.

You are like my **second** family, only **closer**.

"Friendship is the only cement that will ever hold the world together."

WOODROW WILSON

Some **friends** help me to move **house.** **You** help me to move **mountains.**

When I see the world through your eyes, my mind is filled with outrageous possibilities.

Together we can do so much more.

Between **now** and our **destinies,** I **know** you'll be **here.**

Thanks for inviting me over to the sunny side of the street.

I can **depend** on you to be **there** when the **good** times **aren't.**

Even if we're **all** on a **road** to **nowhere,** let's meet up for a **coffee** at the **end.**

"I have no talent for
making new friends
but, oh, such genius
for fidelity to old ones."

Daphne du Maurier

The best thing is, you already know all the reasons why we are friends.

First published by MQ Publications Limited
12 The Ivories
6–8 Northampton Street
London
N1 2HY

Editor: Karen Ball
Design concept: Balley Design Associates
Design: Philippa Jarvis

ISBN: 0-7407-3972-7

Library of Congress Control Number on file

03 04 05 06 07 LEO 10 9 8 7 6 5 4 3 2 1